Alice's Fables

Alice Noriega

AuthorHouse™
1663 Liberty Drive
Bloomington, IN 47403
www.authorhouse.com
Phone: 833-262-8899

Because of the dynamic nature of the Internet, any web addresses or links contained in this book may have changed
since publication and may no longer be valid. The views expressed in this work are solely those of the author and do not
necessarily reflect the views of the publisher, and the publisher hereby disclaims any responsibility for them.

Any people depicted in stock imagery provided by Getty Images are models,
and such images are being used for illustrative purposes only.
Certain stock imagery © Getty Images.

This book is printed on acid-free paper.

ISBN: 978-1-4567-4987-3 (sc)
ISBN: 978-1-4772-0748-2 (e)

Library of Congress Control Number: 2011903601

Print information available on the last page.

Published by AuthorHouse 03/28/2024

Dedication

To my many grandchildren and my five greats.

To the many little rugrats out there, I hope that you may also enjoy this book.

The Little Fat Frog

Once I was a little frog who ate so much they named me Hog, the lily's in the pond I could not jump so there I would sit on a log watching my brother's and sisters frolic with the little polliwog's.

Then as darkness began closing in I sat and I cried because I could not swim, these tears that fell upon this log were sounds that were saying. "Listen little Hog! Jump off that log and spring those legs up that hill every day, and you will be back in the pond swimming with glee! He is no longer a Hog, that is our little family frog!

"The Very Big Tree"

When I was a little tot mom showed me how to plant a twig that one day may be bigger than me.

Every morning I would run out back to see if this twig was getting bigger than me, becoming discouraged my interest went back to riding my bike up those hills out back.

As time moved on I became a young man that now has a tot of my own, yes I am a daddy now and told him the story how mom told me of the twig that one day may be bigger than me. His eye's grew large as he yelled out loud wow wee!!

While visiting mom one bright summer day, I said hey mom! Have you still got that little bike in the shed out back!! She replied, "Yes son and be careful of that big huge tree that once a little tot planted for me.

"A Frighten Baby Bird"

Walking through a field of very high grass, a sound I heard. And yes it was a chirruping baby bird.

Very frighten when it saw me, my thought was to pick it up and take it home, to comfort it from being alone, and possibly harmed.

When out of the blue came two adult birds in a circular motion above my head, chirruping, and diving as if to say, thank you young man please be on your way, yes that is our baby now you have a nice day!

"My Dog Rag's and My Red Wagon"

Rag's had a favorite stuffed teddy bear, that he would carry with him every where, never let it out of sight, also slept with every night.

One afternoon while pulling my red wagon up a hill, it began to feel a little heavy to pull, I stopped and turned, and there was Rag's sitting in my wagon with his teddy bear in his mouth, looking at me with those big brown eye's, as if to say, I have a family, I am no longer a stray, I love you and my teddy more, and more every day!

"The Abandon Little Kitty"

Do you have a little kitty, or a cat? I found my kitty as a tiny baby all alone in the cold out back.

I picked it up then hurried inside for mom to see, mom said that poor little kitty is shivering and cold, also hungry I am sure.

Quickly I ran to the refrigerator for some milk, and mom said sonny this little kitty is too small to learn to drink by it self.

Mom went to the medicine chest to find an eye dropper syringe, she washed it, warmed some milk, cradled the kitty with a towel and began to feed it like a new born baby, and to my surprise it opened its tiny eye's and anxiously put it's little tiny paws around the syringe and began to drink it's milk.

Mom said this little kitty needs a name sonny! I said mom it is black let's call him Jet ok? Mom said sorry this is a little girl, how will Jetta sound dear?

"When It Rains"

On a rainy day we must play inside to keep us dry, we wonder why it rains. Sometimes mother nature has her way!

Without the rain we would have no water, no lakes, no rivers and the ocean may go dry.

The beautiful colors of the flowers that dance in the spring need a drink of water as you, and I, so we don't go dry!

Without the rain the grass would not grow, the sheep, cows, and many animals depend on this grass as a medication to stay well!

"My New Little Baby Brother"

I was very excited when I learned I was to be a big brother very soon, now I will not be just me, and at times very, very lonely.

Being the big brother I will have a lot of responsibility's teaching little brother how to brush his teeth, wash his hands, not to throw sand, to understand the dangers along the way.

I shall save him my skates gosh!! I can hardly wait! I will have to tell Jake our little dog about our new family member on the way when we play!

"The Easter Bunny is Coming"

Do you know the Easter Bunny? I am sure you do. He is that bunny that hides all those beautiful colored eggs for you.

This is called an Easter egg hunt, lots of little girls and boy's join in with their baskets and began to search to find those pretty colored eggs in the tall grass that Mr. Bunny hides away.

When I was a little girl I would cry because I did not find many egg's like some, and mom would say listen! Little one if you only found one beautiful easter egg be happy and say happy Easter to all I had a fun day!

"My New Birthday Puppy"

Today is my birthday and now I am five, I heard mom say come quick inside and you will see a great surprise!

As I ran into the house I saw a very large box wiggling with sounds of arf, arf, my eyes opened wide as I opened the flaps to see this little black and white puppy wagging his tiny tail and wimpering yaps.

Very excited I grabbed his front paw to pick him up and he began to cry mom said now you must be very careful with your new little puppy and give him lots of love and you will see this puppy a buddy he will always be.

Mom said what will you name your new puppy son? It is your birthday and you are now five how about big five sonny?

www.ingramcontent.com/pod-product-compliance
Lightning Source LLC
Chambersburg PA
CBHW060828290526
45792CB00005BB/1837